THE BUCK *STILL* STOPS NOWHERE

**Why America's Health Care is All Dollars
and No Sense and What You Can Do To Change It**

3rd Edition

BY

KATHLEEN O'CONNOR

Cover and Book Design by Vladimir Verano, Third Place Press

Cover image: © S.K.O'donnell via istockphoto.com

THIRD EDITION

ISBN: 978-0-9909926-0-8

Published by:
Kathleen O'Connor
www.oconnorreport.com
kathleen@oconnorreport.com

Printed by Third Place Press
Lake Forest Park, Washington
www.thirdplacepress.com

Praise for *The Buck Still Stops Nowhere*

Kathleen O'Connor's updated *The Buck Stops Nowhere* is a great place for Americans to familiarize themselves with the major flaws in our health care system. And no one attacks this set of problems with more passion and integrity.

~Edward Howard, Executive Vice President, Alliance for Health Reform, Washington DC

Kathleen O'Connor brings fresh insights to a topic long covered up by industry insiders. Health care reporting becomes clear and incisive in her hands. She speaks for the average person lost in the complications of health care policy, and she does so with clarity and courage.

~James Vesely, Editorial Page Editor, The *Seattle Times*, retired

As the premier business magazine in Washington State, we wanted a person who could cover difficult health subjects, especially the complicated and elusive insurance industry. Even health care officials who did not like having the light of a magazine article shined on them had to agree O'Connor got her facts straight. I received many calls from unhappy health care executives, but it always turned out that they were unhappy she told the story, rather than any inaccuracies. If you want someone to say it like it is and get it right every time, then you want to read Kathleen O'Connor.

~Jack Mayne, Editor and Publisher, Washington CEO Magazine, retired

Finally! A book that cuts through the complexity and gets to the heart of the matter—safety and quality for everyone.

~RADM Herb M.Bridge, USNR (ret) United States Navy, Co-Chairman, Ben Bridge Jewelers

*This book is dedicated to the memory of my son Remi Miles Kaemke
November 7, 1978—December 22, 1991*

*and to Karen Ferrier who made the call that saved my life. She died
August 27, 2014.*

*To: Station Six and Engine Six, Seattle Fire Department
Emergency Room and ICU staff at Harborview Medical Center*

*To all the good people in the health care system who try their best
often against all odds.*

ACKNOWLEDGEMENTS

My safe return to health would not have been possible without so many people. The neurology team at Harborview and my Orange Team who pushed me back to health, even though they told me not to write. I owe them much of my return to a normal life.

First Karen Ferrier who told people where to find relatives and personal information I did not have in order. Marsha Thomas, a staunch and fearless advocate who had health care power of attorney; my cousin Vandra Linder who answered questions only a blood relative could; Wanda Morgan, Condo manager, Liz and Gene Brandzel, who found the power of attorney papers and the impossible lists of relatives and friends and who kept my home affairs organized and clean; Jeri "Cookie" Wenke, who walked me from sickness back to health with compassion and humor and made sure I was safe at home.

Sandy Walker MD, Debbie Killinger and Lynn Ryder who jumped in to make sure I was taken care of and who reached out to friends to let them know what happened. Lynn died in January 2015 and was key in organizing a group of anonymous donors to help with my medical expenses my insurance did not cover. She also gave me my start in health care so many years ago.

Shirley Bridge who taught me women really can and must speak up. Marjorie Chadsey, a staunch undying friend. We share a passion that the public has a critical voice in health care. My poetry and reading groups since the 1970's and so many friends who wrapped their arms around me—took me shopping, to appointments, to lunch and brought me meals. And gave me books so I could regain my ability to follow stories, understand and thoughtfully and cogently read again. No thanks would be complete without recognizing the seamless efforts and love of John and Mary Campbell and their family who have included me as their own.

No acknowledgement would be complete without recognizing my neurologist, Dr. Podemski who listened—and acted—on what I said I needed. And my new primary care doctor, Dr.Detering and my great therapy team at Group Health—Joe, Michele and Petra who kept insisting I try harder. My many thanks for pushing me.

This may be overly long, but when you stare death in the face, you realize how precious people are and the difference people make in your life.

INTRODUCTION

I am stunningly lucky to be alive. I suffered a stroke in January 2014 but my type of stroke has an 80 to 90 percent recovery rate. I was on the floor of my home for two days before friends could reach the manager to have her check on me because I was not answering my phone or e-mails. The manager called 911. The EMT team rushed me to Harborview, a regional medical center. I was yellow, black and blue over my entire body. I was barely breathing. Neither the medics nor the ER physicians expected me to live.

I had incredible care from excellent health care professionals. I had robust health insurance through Medicare. I have strong and close networks of friends and colleagues who shouldered me through. And, I know the health care system. Too many are not blessed with such gifts for support, which is why I am updating my earlier book—being a patient brought a greater personal immediacy and a deeper understanding of our system's significant flaws. I have the support, coverage, friends, colleagues and knowledge. Even with all these gifts I still faced problems.

I had excellent care but still the ball was still dropped somewhere between my hospital stay and outpatient care. I had an extraordinary and savvy advocate while I was in the hospital. She watched over me like a hawk to make sure I was well taken care of and spoke for me when I could not. She made sure I made it to appointments on time and helped organize and manage my medications when I returned home. I had friends who ran the gauntlet of the system to make sure I had the best of care. Yet I still had to make decisions and was faced with forms and bills I still do not understand. I did not realize what was covered and not covered by my supplemental insurance. Because I was so near death I was taken to a hospital that was not a contract hospital with my insurance. I signed the form that I 'knew' this was a 'non-contract' hospital for stroke care. I feared for months for the bill that I knew would surely come. It never came. This is now a year later.

I was labeled as anxious by both the hospital and the assisted living facility because I wanted to understand and know my medications. There were so many white pills. How do I know I have the right pill? How do I know if the dose is correct? I thought I was fact checking.

Medicare covered not only my hospital care but my rehabilitation care. For those without Medicare lack of rehabilitation care can be a devastating personal and financial blow because rehabilitation coverage is so limited. Without adequate rehabilitation patients don't improve. Financially I would have been devastated if it were not for a group of anonymous friends. Assisted living is not covered by Medicare. Like so many others I could have faced medical bankruptcy from my bills if it were not for these friends and my pharmaceutical coverage through Medicare. My co-payment for one anti-seizure medication was $278 nearly every month. I was on three anti-seizure medications.

Because of the stroke I could not work to supplement my bare bones retirement. I would have possibly qualified for Social Security Disability but that can take up to a year to be approved. I managed to pay my mortgage. Too many others can't.

I know the system. I speak English and know the culture. I had excellent insurance and had enough financial resources and assistance to survive. I had a good education. I am not afraid to ask questions or challenge authority. Too many others don't. Too many are harmed physically and financially.

Therefore, I cannot remain silent as attempt after attempt is made to dismantle the Affordable Care Act. There are deep systemic health care problems in our health care system that must not be ignored. We must take these first steps to move forward so we can have safe, accountable and affordable health care. This won't happen overnight, but it must be done or we will remain in the same unaccountable, incomprehensible and unaffordable morass outlined in this intentionally brief book.

This guide is just a quick introduction. If it seems confusing and tedious that is because the system is confusing and tedious. If the guide seems incomprehensible, redundant and littered with gaps and duplications, that is because the system is incomprehensible, redundant and littered with gaps and duplications. If this guide seems senseless that is because the system is senseless.

I told myself when my son died in 1991: "When the worst thing that can happen to you has happened it changes how you calculate risk." I can't do much but I can write.

As someone once told me: "Fate is the cards you are dealt. Free will is how you play your hand." I write to play my hand.

A CLEAR CONCISE GUIDE TO AMERICA'S HEALTH CARE

- Health Care is foreign territory. Unlike foreign countries there is no embassy or safe haven.

- What you pay depends on where you live, your insurance and where you work.

- Insurance rules are different in each state.

- Even federal programs like Medicare have different rates and fees in each state including physician fees.

- Medicaid, which is a joint program between the federal government and the states, has different coverage, costs and fees in each state.

- There are no consistent or constant rules. Federal and state policies shift constantly.

- Insurance rules in one state do not apply in another.

- • Nearly 400,000 die annually from medical errors at a cost of $1 trillion.

- There are no consistent, predictable costs and no way for anyone to compare them.

- Nothing is constant.

- The only two words that apply to the health care system are:

  It Depends.

SOME BRIGHT LIGHT IN A DARK TUNNEL:

SAFETY, QUALITY AND OUTCOMES

- Hospitals are now accountable for safety, quality, value and outcomes. They are fined if quality and outcomes are poor. Those results are publically reported.

- Hospitals are now also accountable to their communities for community health needs. They can be fined $50,000 for not doing so.

- Hospitals must now have community representatives on their boards and publish and promote their financial aid policies.

- Hospitals must also work with doctors to send one bill to patients for both doctor and hospital services.

- Doctors are held equally accountable and must report conflicts of interest, such as accepting payments from pharmaceutical companies for speaking engagements and continuing medical education subsidized by pharmaceutical companies.

- Doctors and hospitals must work together in Accountable Care Organizations (ACOs) to focus on quality patient care. They must also eliminate unnecessary tests and procedures.

- Pharmaceutical and medical device companies are now taxed on their profits to help pay for changes introduced in the Affordable Care Act.

- Health insurance companies cannot limit a patient's lifetime expenses or turn someone away because of a pre-existing condition.

- Skilled nursing homes that receive Medicare and Medicaid funds must disclose information on ownership, accountability requirements and expenses. This information will be posted on a website so patients and families can compare them.

These new requirements are being fought in the courts, in the states and in Congress.

SOME PROMISING EXAMPLES

Major national non-partisan groups exist as advocates and educators on health care reform, such as the Alliance for Health Reform, the National Coalition for Health Care and the Institute for Health Improvement among many others.

State wide groups, such as the Foundation for Health Care Quality and the Washington Health Alliance in Washington are just two state examples that examine the system, advocate for safety and quality and identify ways to act on them. There are many others.

National and state business coalitions formed to influence the health care marketplace. Increasingly these employer groups are focusing on quality, outcomes and value as a way to lower costs and improve patient care. Their assumption is that better quality will lower costs and increase value.

The best known national players are The Leapfrog Group, the National Business Group on Health and the Pacific Business Group on Health which include private Fortune 500 companies, other large employers, federal, state and local purchasers of health care. They use their purchasing power to influence the marketplace to increase safety, value and accountability.

Private foundations such as the Commonwealth Fund, Kaiser Family Foundation, Robert Wood Johnson Foundation and RAND Health have conducted research studies for years on various aspects of the health care system. There are many others, such as the California Health Foundation, California Wellness Foundation and the Northwest Health Foundation in Portland, Oregon.

These groups and their approaches don't make headlines but they contribute more to improve patient care and lower costs than other stop gap reactive measures.

The law of unintended consequences, however, brought us to where we are today. Mistakes and cost increases have been caused by both political parties.

THE BASICS

Without a shared goal for our health care system, costs, rules and regulations are driven by different and conflicting forces:

1. Health insurance is not considered commerce and therefore has been regulated by the states since 1869 with the first of several Supreme Court decisions.

2. There are no national safety or benefit standards for health care. Therefore there are 50 different state rules, not counting the rules of different agencies responsible for various aspects of health care from private insurance to public employers, unions, corporations, small businesses, workers compensation, and so forth.

3. Employers with 100 or more people can 'self fund' their health care benefits. They are not considered 'insurance companies' and are therefore exempt from state insurance regulations. Beginning in 2017, they are subject to some taxes on health benefits.

There are no consistent rules and regulations. This patchwork quilt has led to a proliferation of agencies and regulations that overlap and duplicate. These redundancies and duplications create higher costs.

HOW THIS HAPPENED

Health insurance has been exempt from meaningful national standards since the beginning of health insurance. The 1869 Supreme Court decision found that insurance was not commerce and therefore not subject to federal regulation. Insurance regulation was left to the states. This regulatory authority remains today and was validated in the current Dodd-Frank Act. This state by state regulation was a major frustration to large multi-state employers which led in part to their move to self-fund their health benefits which exempts them from state taxes, rules and regulations.

Since World War II our health care has been a form of employee compensation. This model created an irreparably flawed and fragmented system of costs and benefits. Therefore we lack an integrated system of care which led to redundancies and duplications that is littered with gaps, deficiencies, and needs.

With few exceptions, we have no shared health care goals for communities, states or as a nation. The Affordable Care Act is an attempt to change that but it faces entrenched special interest after special interest and a vast political divide even though both Republican and Democratic policies raised costs.

In 2013, 48 percent of all Americans had insurance through their employer. (*http://kff.org/other/state-indicator/ total-population/*) This includes public and private employers. The chart includes data by state and coverage by Medicare and Medicaid.

Employer based insurance has been declining from nearly 70 percent in 2003. Employers want to offer health insurance for their employees at the best possible price. When costs get out of line, however, employers put out bids for new estimates to 'control' costs. Until recently there has been no economic incentive for prevention because employers don't want to invest in something that yields benefit to other insurers or companies.

American health care policy, therefore, focuses solely on costs and who is going to pay for it. Only recently have quality, safety and outcomes come into the picture.

HERE IS HOW THE 'SYSTEM' WORKS AND WHY IT IS NO LONGER EFFECTIVE.

Because we have no goal for a health care system we have perverse incentives that pit one group against another for economic survival. The Affordable Care Act is a good step in the right direction but there are few vocal advocates. The public, therefore, is lost in the lurch.

Our health care system is like an amoeba. When costs decline in one area increases erupt in another. The traditional way to pay for health care was simply to pay what doctors and hospitals charged. The so-called "fee-for-service" approach. This approach has absolutely no brakes on costs. Doctors and hospitals could set their own rates and the rates for the technology they used. Hospitals used to keep patients as long as they liked and charged what they needed to cover their costs. Doctors were paid every time they saw a patient. Both could set their own rates and see their patients for as long and as frequently as they wanted.

This employee compensation model of health care created a 'use it or lose' it mentality of use and benefits. It pits large employers against the small, the individuals, unions, the old and the poor. They all also play by different rules.

The current focus on value, outcomes, safety and quality promises to change our costly piecemeal approach to lower costs, but it is a long and winding road.

The new national Essential Benefits package was designed to guarantee the same health coverage no matter where someone works, unless they work in a self-funded company. Such coverage means people are no longer tied to jobs just to keep their health care benefits and are no longer caught in the so-called 'job-lock' that kept people in jobs for fear of losing their health care benefits when they or a family member needed them.

Even with the Affordable Care Act large self-funded employers do not have to offer the Essential Benefits. Nor do they have to justify rate increases or have to spend 80 percent of their 'health care premium' costs on employee health care services.

EMPLOYERS

While some forms of health insurance existed in the US it was not until World War II that American employers assumed their dominant role. With the wage-price freeze employers could not give raises to attract or reward employees. Consequently, employers such as Kaiser Shipyard lobbied to offer health insurance in lieu of wages. This eventually led to three things: 1) health care benefits were not subject to wage and price controls; 2) health insurance and other employee benefits were subject to collective bargaining and 3) in the 1950's the IRS ruled that health insurance premiums paid by employers could come from pre-tax dollars and were therefore exempt from corporate income tax

These practices continue to the present day. Health care as employee compensation still dominates our health care. Americans lucky enough to have employer paid care, however, began to lose touch with the cost of health care services because most of those services were paid by their employer. Expansion of health care benefits in lieu of wage increases occurred in both FDR's and Nixon's administrations.

Any change in the health care system, therefore, must suit the needs of employers or at least not harm or alarm them. This is one reason the Affordable Care Act focused first on the uninsured individuals, Medicaid expansion, small businesses and individuals for fear of angering large employers.

Health care benefits for these large employers are exempt from state insurance laws, state mandated benefits and state insurance premium taxes. It used to be that only the largest of employers could afford the risk of this 'self insurance.' Now companies as small as 100 employees can afford to self insure with stop loss insurance. Self insurance also erases a revenue stream that would otherwise go into state budget coffers.

Small employers and individuals remain at the mercy of commercial insurance companies with standard, off-the-shelf benefit packages that are subject to state insurance taxes, rules and regulations. While state insurance packages must include the new Essential Benefits, small business still face higher per capita costs even with the Affordable Care Act because the insurance company can set its own rates based on its provider network costs.

Small businesses are also pounded by the way insurance risk pools work. Smaller risk pools mean the cost of one person's illness is spread over a smaller group of people. This increases costs for everyone in that company. Costs are based on the health status of everyone inside the company. Smaller groups have higher risks and potentially higher costs. Larger groups lower individual costs and therefore lower rates. Small businesses also pay much higher per capita administrative costs. When it comes to health policy laws and regulations, however, small businesses often follow the lobbying lead of big business.

Having one Essential Benefits package offers the promise of reducing the complexity of health care benefits and the chance of lowering health care costs, even though a variety of choices remain that can be added to Essential Benefits.

Not only are employers the major player in health insurance, they also have many groups to help sculpt health care benefit options. The work of these companies is included in insurance premium costs.

ACTUARIES, BROKERS, AND BENEFIT CONSULTING FIRMS

An entire industry exists to sculpt, interpret and sell health care benefits for businesses and individuals. Three major groups assist with this effort: employee benefit consulting firms, actuaries and brokers.

Employee Benefit Consulting Firms design benefit packages based on how employers want to balance cost and employee satisfaction. One firm, Mercer LLC is the world's largest employee benefit consulting firm, now owned by Marsh McLennan.

Not only do these firms design benefit packages they also conduct research on the impact of benefit designs. They can demonstrate the difference in use and cost, for example, by changing a co-payment from $10 to $15. Their salaries and commissions are included in health care premium costs.

Actuaries determine the odds of how many people in a group will get sick and use services and put a price on that information. A small hair salon with largely young females, and therefore at risk of childbearing, will pay a higher price than a gas station with equally young males. Ranchers and farmers pay more than accounting firms because they are subject to more physical hazards.

Actuaries also calculate the odds of health or illness, put a price on those odds and call that "premiums." Their salaries and commissions are also included in health care premium dollars.

Brokers save the buyer—the employer or individual—the trouble of comparison shopping. They ask what the buyer wants, investigate the market, then return with options. Like a realtor they receive a percentage of the sale. Their commissions are also included in premium costs. Their commissions and sales incentives vary by insurance company. It's often buyer-beware because a broker may be more enthusiastic about insurers that pay a larger commission.

Employers were initially generous with benefits and cost subsidies. The trend for the past 20 years as health care costs have consumed larger and larger percentages of an employer's budget is to shift more and more costs to employees in the form of higher premiums, co-payments, higher out of pocket maximum costs and higher deductibles.

Large multi-state employers are driven wild by the different rules and regulations and networks and benefit options in each and every state. Yet, they resist uniform or standard benefits because they believe it takes away their ability to compete for the best employees.

OTHER EMPLOYER RELATED INSURANCE GROUPS AND ORGANIZATIONS.

MEWAS (Multiple Employer Welfare Associations) permit some small employers to band together to purchase more affordable benefits for their employees often across state lines.

Association Health Plans and Trusts also permit groups of employers in the same industry to band together to offer insurance to certain groups, such as construction workers and even city and county workers. Many of these plans are under review at the state level to see if they meet the Affordable Care Act's requirements.

WORKERS' COMPENSATION PROGRAMS

Each state has a pooled worker's compensation program for employers to share the costs of employees who are hurt on the job. Employers pay into the fund so such injuries do not fall exclusively on one company alone. Because they are state programs, benefits are determined and funded on a state by state basis. They are, however, regulated by the US Department of Labor. There are some clinics that focus solely on caring for patients who are injured at work. These clinics don't necessarily communicate with regular practices or hospitals, and vice versa.

Employers were the originators of health care as an employee benefit even though there were also early union plans, such as those for railroad workers and seamen.

UNIONS AND UNION TRUSTS

Unions were the early advocates that brought health insurance to the workplace. Some created their own plans, started clinics for their members and fought for health insurance coverage for their members. Since the mid-1940s health insurance benefits have become a part of the labor contracts. Strikes around the country often include healthcare benefits as they were in the 2009 United Auto Workers negotiations with Ford and the 2000 labor negotiations between Boeing and the Machinist Union.

Unlike the self-funded companies they work for unions are subject to the provisions of the Affordable Care Act.

Over the years unions have gone from being advocates for their members who did not have insurance to often insisting on some of the nation's most generous health care benefits. This has eroded the broad public support they once enjoyed. Union demands that their members not share in premium costs or pay deductibles do not sit well with the non-unionized public that faces increasing out of pocket costs and higher deductibles.

Some recent strikes, however, have been about health care costs, recruiting low paid non-union workers, such as home health care workers, and greater workplace safety, such as the Steelworkers' strike in Texas and Oklahoma and the Nurses strike over patient safety and staffing in California.

Taft-Hartley Plans are another form of insurance available for union members even though the employee may work for a company that offers health care benefits. A large national company such as Safeway may offer its employees several different benefit packages, one of which is a union trust, which further muddies the water. In 2013 union workers represented 11 percent of all workers. The rate for the private sector was nearly 7 percent and the public sector 35 percent. These numbers are subject to change as more and more states battle over Right to Work laws which do not require workers to join unions or pay union dues to work in some industries or public sector jobs.

The shifting sands of health change constantly. By the time this book is published rules will have changed again and more coverage will be denied, altered or added.

HOSPITALS

Hospitals account for nearly 40 percent of all health care costs including inpatient and outpatient care. It is the single largest cost sector of the health care economy. There are nearly 6,000 public and private hospitals.

Medicare paid hospitals by the number of days a patient spent in a hospital. This caused tremendous cost increases. That method changed in the 1980s with the Prospective Payment system and DRGs (Diagnostic Related Groups). The new reimbursement was based on a patient's disease and condition. Medicare payments matter because they represent about 30 percent of all hospital income—even up to 50 percent in rural areas because they have fewer providers and more elderly, poor and uninsured patients.

Because of its dominant role Medicare also drives the commercial marketplace. Private insurers find it easier to follow Medicare payment patterns than to create their own.

The DRG payment system sent hospital administrators frantically searching for ways to replace what had been a very lucrative fee for service revenue stream. They began marketing.

The marketing focused first on women. "Birthing Centers" erupted around the country because women make 75 percent of all health care decisions. If a woman was happy with her maternity experience she would most likely organize the family's health care around that hospital and the doctors who had admitting privileges there. The marketing worked even though many maternity centers were "loss leaders" if they didn't deliver enough babies.

Maternity centers are now big business. In many places normal vaginal delivers are declining while C-sections are rising. Normal vaginal deliveries in 2009 cost around $10, 700. A C-section without complications costs were about $18,000. Because many of these C-sections are early, pre-term deliveries many hospitals have also added neo-natal intensive care units. These units raised the cost of care as well as physician and hospital income.

More hospitals also added emergency rooms for the same reasons—more unregulated revenue.

Another consequence of the new DRG payment system was the introduction of out-patient surgery that did not require overnight stays. These same-day outpatient (ambulatory) surgery centers were outside the scope of DRG regulations and generated unregulated income.

More unregulated sources were found in diagnostic tests. Hospitals rushed to buy MRIs, CT (CAT) scanners and other diagnostic equipment. The purchase of this equipment, however, generated pressure for patients to use the equipment so hospitals could pay off their investments.

The very things that created income for hospitals, however, created conflict with physicians because many of those out-patient services had been performed by physicians. Therefore, physicians decided that if patients no longer needed to stay overnight in a hospital then physicians could do same-day surgery as easily as hospitals. And, if the hospitals could have diagnostic equipment then so could physician practices. Hence the introduction of 'facility fees.'

And so the duplication goes on and costs go up.

Doctors and hospitals who were once largely partners became competitors for many of the same services. Duplication became rampant. Physicians and physician groups, however, could not compete with deep pocket hospitals. Doctors once had mostly private practices. Now over 50 percent of all physicians are now hospital employees. Some investor-owned hospitals can now also reap IRS tax benefits by employing physicians.

To protect themselves against readmission fines, hospitals are now billing for 'observation' care. Observation care is technically not a "readmission" for which hospitals are now being fined. Because Medicare requires a two day 'hospital' stay for patients to qualify for skilled nursing care coverage, patients now face paying for the skilled nursing care themselves because 'observation care' is not considered a hospital 'admission.'

Hospitals are now hiring a new type of physician employee called 'Hospitalists.' Hospitalists oversee a patient's hospital care once a patient has been admitted to a given hospital. Hospitalists have no interaction with the patient prior to admission but are in charge of the patient's care rather than the private physician patients have in the community. Frequently, the patient's physician is excluded from care decisions even though they have treated the patient and family for twenty plus years.

Many think the days of a primary care personal physician as patient advocate are dying rapidly. Patients or their advocates have to "coordinate" the care and make sure communication among specialists, hospitalists and primary care physicians happens or even works when a patient is most vulnerable. This is often a challenge even for those who know the health care system and an impenetrable morass for those outside the medical community.

A major problem especially for single patients or for many patients who have no children, living or near-by blood relatives is HIPAA (Health Insurance Portability and Accountability Act). While well intended from some early concerns, such as HIV positive status it can and does leave patients vulnerable about sharing their health histories or have others speak for them when they cannot. Unless friends or relatives are specifically designated, friends cannot speak for or ask about a patient. It is illegal for health professionals to share patient health care information.

This includes parents of adult children simply because their child is over the age of 18 and therefore is technically no longer a child.

A major marketplace reaction to the DRG payment system was the introduction of Managed Care. Physicians were to be in groups that would coordinate patient care and have one physician be responsible for coordinating care for a given patient. While that original approach 'failed' with the so called 'Hillary Care' it has become a major force within the insurance industry and a key influence behind the new Accountable Care Organizations (ACOs) in the Affordable Care Act. The Affordable Care Act has teeth to reward hospitals and physicians for patient outcomes which was not part of the earlier approach. The ACOs are responsible for both inpatient and out-patient outcomes, safety and value. The earlier focus stressed volume not quality for financial rewards.

Accountable Care Organizations are responsible for reducing costs by encouraging doctors, hospitals and other health care providers to form networks that provide efficient quality care, value to patients and quality outcomes. Providers in these networks are eligible for Medicare bonuses for their performance.

Most hospitals are non-profit organizations and are required by the IRS to offer community benefit, to conduct searches for comparable CEO salaries, and to cover the costs for the uninsured. Hospitals have as many prices for drugs, procedures and services as there are insurance companies. Uninsured people get hit the hardest with the top prices because they have no access to any discounts. The Affordable Care Act did tackle this issue with some success. Most CEO's to date, however, are not held accountable for patient care or outcomes.

Another major requirement of the Accountable Care Act is hospital fines for poor quality care. Hospitals are now fined and identified for safety errors, poor quality of care and outcomes, unnecessary re-admissions and hospital acquired infections.

The new emphasis on quality and value requires hospitals to conduct Community Health Needs Assessments (CHNAs) and to publically promote their financial assistance policies. Failure to do so can cost $50,000 in fines and the potential loss of a hospital's non-profit 501(c)(3) status.

Hospitals are also accountable to their communities through community engagement, largely known as "population health." Hospitals must now report not only on their community health activity, but how they must address those health care needs. People from the community must serve on their boards of directors. If hospitals have more than one facility the Affordable Care Act provision applies to all those facilities as well. The hospital's Board of Directors is responsible for all the hospitals' activities, safety, financial assistance and community reports.

Changing the health care system is no simple act. It alone accounts for nearly 20 percent of the US economy. The changes over the years have largely been reactions to revenue streams not on quality of care and patient safety and outcomes. Different payment systems, however, have wreaked havoc on patients, hospitals and physicians. Until we have one common approach we will live on constantly shifting sands leaving consumers afraid for their lives with shorter hospital stays, more safety concerns, poorer quality and higher costs.

Even with its warts and all, the Affordable Care Act and its emphasis on patient safety and quality outcomes, and penalty fines for hospitals and doctors is fresh air. It is the first promise of a new foundation that links safety and quality of care to payment.

DOCTORS

Doctors have often resisted reform efforts. The doctor's professional association, American Medical Association (AMA), opposed the recommendations of the 1932 Committee on the Costs of Medical Care which called for community health planning and salaried physicians. They were early opponents of cooperative physician practices like those of the Mayo Clinic and Kaiser Health plans. In 1942 they took the issues of salaried physicians to the US Supreme Court which ruled against the AMA in 1943 and allowed physicians to be salaried by private employers or in other group practices.

Up until the advent of the DRG's in the 1980's, hospitals and doctors could largely set their own fees. The DRG payment system for hospitals also brought about payment changes doctors accepted for Medicare and Medicaid patients. This has created a new war zone.

All physician income is not the same. The hope was to adjust physician fees to eliminate the large rate differences between specialists—such as cardiologists and neurosurgeons—and primary care family doctors and pediatricians. These formulas are known as RBRVS (Resource Based Relative Value System) and later the SGR's (Sustainable Growth Rates). Fights about these rates erupt annually.

Until the late 90's, nearly 50 percent of all physicians were in single or double office practices—a physician or a physician and a partner. As medical models and payments structures changed more and more physicians joined or started group practices. Most of these are referred to as Medical Group Practices that range in size and complexity from smaller groups, to a Mayo

Clinic and large physician group practices in large metropolitan centers.

Since the beginning of the decade individual practices have decreased. Group practices have grown and now nearly 50 percent of all doctors are salaried professionals in group practices or have been hired by hospitals.

After the DRG's physicians faced the same dilemma as hospitals—how to replace revenue that drastically decreased because of new hospital out-patient practices. Physician groups began acting more like hospitals and began buying equipment and offering tests at their clinics for patient convenience and revenue. This increased the volume of patient visits, procedures and income. Some even began offering outpatient surgery and added new costs called 'facility fees.'

The Affordable Care Act now focuses on Accountable Care Organizations that require hospitals and doctors to work together to provide patient value. How these new organizations will evolve with their new networks and the new value focus is not yet realized. Trusted and collaborative partnerships are hard to master in a traditionally competitive environment.

What is not commonly recognized is that competition in health care drives up costs for the system as a whole. For example, if every hospital and physician group in a city has a CT scan machine, they all need to drive patients to use those machines to recoup the cost of their investments. Consequently, patients often receive tests they may not need. At $250,000-plus for an MRI or CT scan machines, many patients are needed to pay off these investments. The financial incentive, therefore, is to order the tests.

The prices for services, however, are anyone's guess. Prices are determined by overhead, salaries, infrastructure, local taxes and profits. Most physician practices are for profit, unless they are tied to hospitals and have worked out a payment structure with them. Prices are virtually impossible for consumers to decipher. Choices are often limited to the network people are in and so many prices are determined also by who is paying for the service and the community in which people live.

In terms of total costs, physician and clinic visits account for nearly 25 percent of all health care costs.

Physician influence in health care reform is significant, however. There are over one million licensed physicians and over 800,000 currently in practice. They excerpt tremendous influence in health care reform because of their numbers and their wealth as both individuals and as national, state and county organizations such as the AMA and state and county medical societies. Their opposition to reform that promises to threaten their independent practices has been long term and profound.

NURSES

Nurses are passionate patient advocates. Hospitals and doctors, however, often have a love hate relationship with them. Insurers love them because they are cheaper than doctors. In 2015, Nebraska became the 20th state to allow ARNP's (Advance Registered Nurse Practitioners) to practice without a doctor's supervision. Nurses also have unions that strike over quality of care, wages and terms and conditions of employment. The American Nurses Association is both a professional association and a union. This distinguishes them from doctors who are not unionized.

To lower costs in the past many hospitals didn't hire enough experienced skilled nurses. Many hospitals also required mandatory overtime. Some of this is changing. Nursing care faces challenges as patients are sicker with more complex care needs. These care demands come at a time when there are fewer qualified nurses to provide services. Nurses are now older—the average age of hospital nurses is forty-six—many are thinking about retiring. Nursing care also takes physical tolls as well. Care requires lifting and turning patients, many of whom are now obese.

A nurse is not just a nurse. Nursing degrees range from ARNP (Advance Registered Nurse Practitioner) who can often prescribe medications, to RN (Registered Nurse) to NP (nurse practitioner). All have different practice guidelines and scopes of practice rules. Nursing care is no longer restricted primarily to hospitals as more people age into skilled nursing homes and assisted living facilities that require extensive nursing care.

This need for nurses will only increase as America ages. Increasing age is the best predictor of increasing hospital use. With fewer people choosing nursing as a career a looming care crisis faces baby boomers.

INSURANCE

If a vote were taken on the villain of health care it would probably be a tie between insurers and pharmaceutical companies. Insurers probably lead because of their ever-present and pervasive role. They control the services people get, how people get them, the hospitals and doctors people see, how hospitals, doctor and services are paid and they set the rates for products and services.

Insurance companies are regulated at the state level for the benefits they can offer, their rates, their solvency and their networks. Until the Affordable Care Act there was no one standard benefit package in each state, much less across state lines. A major change in the Affordable Care Act is the requirement for all insurers to offer Essential Benefits. They are also now required to limit their administrative fees to no more than 20 to 25 percent of premium costs depending on employer size.

Longer books can be written about insurance regulations, actions, counter actions, Supreme Court decisions and Congress. Simply put since 1869 when the Supreme Court held that insurance should be free from Commerce Clause regulations insurance regulations have been the province of the states. Occasionally, if not annually, Congress is called upon to change or pre-empt states' rights to regulate insurance, but this state-by-state right remains—and along with it the multi-headed hydra of different state approaches to insurance regulation. This makes the Affordable Care Act implementation challenging, ugly and political, thus stacking more chips against the best interest of people who just want affordable and good quality care.

Not only do insurance companies insure health care benefits, they also own patients' personal health care information such as lab tests results and cell cultures that are paid for by health insurance premium dollars. Personal ownership of personal tissues and parts lost in at least one Supreme Court case. One of the most publicized cases revolved around the cancer cells of a woman named Henrietta Lacks. Her cells were sold at considerable profit to many cancer research laboratories. Her permission and her family's permission were not required and the company/research institute that 'owns' her cells made considerable profit from her cells' success in combating cancer. See: *The Immortal Life of Henrietta Lacks.*

Although insurance companies compete against each other for business they often unite in a flash as legislation intrudes on their autonomy such as some provisions of the Affordable Care Act. While many companies stand to benefit from the Affordable Care Act some of its new requirements impede their ability to practice business as usual. Key changes are: elimination of pre-existing condition clauses; restrictions on profits and administrative costs; the requirement to cover all Essential Benefits and the elimination of financial limits on maximum lifetime costs. While generally supportive of the Affordable Care Act because of the expansion of the number of people who will now be insured, the industry will revert in a flash to former practices given half a chance.

All insurers are not the same which complicates the health care landscape. Insurers are both for-profit and not-for-profit. They are subject to 50 different sets of rules even if they are a national company such as Blue Cross, United Health Care or Aetna. No two insurance regulators have the same view of the Affordable Care Act. We have also seen a sharp divide between Democratic and Republican insurance regulators. No one set of rules applies across the nation except for Medicare. This complexity increases the cost of administration. Even Medicaid has state variations.

The traditional fee-for-service insurers (indemnity) are for-profit. Some not-for-profits, such as Blue Cross and Blue Shield, tried to turn themselves into for-profit enterprises but were prohibited from doing so in some states unless they gave money back to the state for the non-profit tax exempt advantages they enjoyed. That conversion was stopped in its tracks in many states because it became too expensive to pay back the tax advantage of being a non-profit. In California alone, Blue Cross/Blue shield had to pay the state $3.2 billion dollars. Those funds created two state-wide non-profit organizations that focus on health care.

Insurance is a shape-shifting landscape. Few behavioral differences exist, however, between profit and not-for-profit insurers. Not-for-profits have to mimic the behavior and the product designs of the for-profits in order to survive in the same marketplace.

Insurance companies also have myriad products. These products range from the fee-for-service models to HMO models. Even insurance products offered through the Affordable Care Act range from silver to bronze and platinum depending on the generosity of benefits. While they all must cover Essential Benefits, costs often depend on added benefits and the hospitals and doctors that are in the network. If patients go out of the network they must still pay for those services themselves.

The problem remains that virtually no one understands these plans. Even if people do, it doesn't matter. The contracts, networks, and rules change every time plans are renewed and they require fleets of people to stay on top of the different coverage, rules and networks of all the different plans. This increases costs. In the 1990's, for example, one multi-specialty clinic in California with 135 physicians added 25 people full time just to verify the different regulations of 35 different insurance contracts, their different benefits, hospitals and physician networks and patient eligibility. Simply put administrative complexity and frequent plan changes add cost.

Managed care as it was known in the mid-90s was to be the marketplace solution to counter the Clinton health proposal. It was going to save money by focusing on prevention, compiling complex health care information and using computers to save administrative costs. Not only did that fail to materialize, it fell flat on its face because of administrative complexity. Insurers, hospitals and physician practices lost (and continue to lose) millions, if not billions, on failed information systems, dot.coms, eHealth solutions, and now EHR (Electronic Health Records). Electronic medical records (EMRs) still have not delivered on their promise of streamlining or adding efficiency and accuracy in patient care because of the complexity of the differing and constantly changing insurance products that are offered to individuals and employers.

New smart phone APPS may be a promising feature.

Unlike the banking industry, the health care industry has not successfully implemented standard data requirements and reporting. In 1992, the last year of his presidency, President George H.W. Bush called for a national electronic medical record within one year. That goal has yet to be realized.

Prevention? Few insurers wanted to touch it because the average person will be in a health plan at best for three years. Most prevention programs are basically early diagnosis and screening. That said, significant progress on collecting uniform data across physicians and hospitals and reporting comparative quality metric is being made in Washington State by groups such as the Washington Health Care Alliance. (*wahealthalliance.org*) There are many groups in other states. Preventive care is now an Essential Benefit all insurers must provide as part of the Affordable Care Act.

Traditionally the economic incentive for insurance companies was to get as many healthy members as possible to reduce costs. If it was not always possible to get healthy people insurance benefits could be designed to exclude or limit things that sick people use, such as prescription drugs. Some plans excluded maternity care and many excluded mental health. They also add higher deductibles and more patient co-payments for services. While insurance premiums may appear to be more affordable, co-payment, co-insurance, and deductibles increase —thus creating even higher costs for individuals and families.

Even now with the Affordable Care Act that bans the exclusion of pre-existing conditions some insurers simply add higher drug prices that essentially eliminate the higher cost patients who have pre-existing conditions.

Insurers blame consumer groups and state and federal governments for cost increases. They blame legislation that required insurers to cover such things as mammograms or prostate screenings, mental health, or extended stays for maternity care. They blame consumers for being irresponsible users of health care services and causing cost increases, never mentioning that consumers don't pay for those services themselves if they are covered by their employer.

Insurers also blame doctors for wanting too much money, ditto for hospitals. The pharmaceutical industry is now fingered as the cost-increase villain. The only group insurers don't finger are employers who buy their benefits and products.

What is not widely known by the public is that nearly half or more of the "health insurance companies" in the country are "self-insured" employers who act as but are not insurance companies. Large businesses, such as General Motors or Microsoft and many state and local governments are 'self insured.' These employers then hire an insurance company to 'manage' their benefits and claims. Employees, consequently, often have no idea that their company is self-insured because the administrator is an insurance company or its TPA (Third Party Administrator).

Self-insured companies are also exempt from state insurance rules. They are loosely governed by ERISA (Employee Retirement Income Security Act) a national program. They are, therefore, not accountable to or governed by the insurance laws in each individual state. Nor do they pay state premium taxes that commercial insurance companies must pay because they are an employer and not an insurance company.

Self insured companies, at this point, are not required to offer the Essential Benefits or any special benefits in state insurance laws. All this could change if Congress or the courts change or repeal the Affordable Care Act in whole or in part.

Applying the ACA provisions to ERISA companies is significant because it attempts to level the playing field between state regulated plans and ERISA companies. It also assures one core set of benefits and coverage for all companies, despite company size.

Insurance coverage and regulations are complicated by insurance plans that are offered by associations, such as Chambers of Commerce. These "association health plans" are often offered by groups that cross state boundaries, such as MEWA's. These policies are also not subject to state insurance rules and regulations or state insurance premium taxes.

If this is not complicated enough there are also 'public insurance' programs in the form of Medicare and Medicaid.

PUBLIC INSURANCE: MEDICARE AND MEDICAID

Medicare and Medicaid are public insurance programs paid for by our tax dollars, employers and employees and individual contributions. Medicare and Medicaid became law in 1965 to assure the elderly, poor and disabled would have help with their health care costs. In 1965 hospitals were the major cost burden for seniors. Increasingly the major financial burden for seniors is long-term care which Medicare does not cover.

MEDICARE

Medicare originally came in two parts: Medicare Part A and Part B. Medicare Part A covers inpatient hospital costs, some home health care, some skilled nursing care and hospice care. Part B covers services including doctors and other health care professionals, such as certain therapists, home health care, durable medical equipment and some preventive services. Medicare does not cover Assisted Living costs when patients are not sick enough to warrant hospital or skilled nursing care but are too sick or impaired temporarily to live alone and who typically need assistance with personal hygiene, medication management and daily tasks, such meals.

Services not covered by Part A or B can be covered under Medicare supplemental policies from A through F. These policies cover a range of services people can choose from depending on costs and services selected.

These supplemental policies cover items that Medicare does not such as hearing aids and eyeglasses, more extensive rehabilitation care and assisted living, among others. The new Medicare Part C covers private 'Medicare Advantage' plans that are managed care plans offered through employers or by private insurers. Medicare Part D is the new outpatient pharmaceutical benefit. Medicare Parts C and D were passed into law in 2003 at great controversy. For example, it prohibited Medicare to engage in rate negotiations with pharmaceutical companies as the VA can. That responsibility rests with the individual insurance plan. This provision leaves greater financial power to a pharmaceutical company because larger groups like Medicare have more negotiating power than a smaller insurance company with much fewer enrollees.

Part D pharmaceutical coverage can be added to traditional Medicare supplements, some private fee-for-service Medicare plans and Medicare Medical Saving Accounts. Medicare Part D coverage also has a "donut hole" or a temporary limit on drug costs Medicare plans cover. In 2015, once a person or a plan spends $2,960 on prescription medications, the individual will pay 45 percent of the plan's costs for brand-name prescription drugs. Or as Medicare offices describe the "donut hole:"

> *"Although you'll only pay 45% of the price for the brand-name drug in 2015, 97.5% of the price—what you pay plus the 52.2% manufacturer discount payment—will count as out-of-pocket costs which will help you get out of the coverage gap. What the drug plan pays toward the drug cost and toward the dispensing fee isn't counted toward your out-of-pocket spending."*

Clear as mud for individuals trying to understand their financial contributions. For example, between 2002 and 2013 Digoxin—a drug used to treat heart failure—increased in price by 637 percent.

This impenetrable language is not restricted to Medicare.

While Medicare Part A benefits are the same in every state the rates for hospitals, doctors, medications, skilled nursing facilities can vary county by county and supplemental plan by supplemental plan across each and every state. Doctors in California, Arkansas or New York, for example, are paid differently for doing the same medical procedure as doctors in Wyoming, Texas or Illinois.

In short, payment for the same procedure differs state by state by state and even within each state. These rates are not tied to the cost of living. Rather they are tied to the historical rates (called usual and customary rates—(UCR) hospitals and doctors charged in those counties and states. These rates are also governed by something called AAPCC (Average Area Per Capita Costs). This means that hospitals and physicians in the most expensive areas of the country receive the most money

Congress not only sets Medicare rates for hospitals, doctors, home health care, nursing homes and even medical equipment, it also decides the services Medicare covers. It literally took an act of Congress to cover mammograms and prostate screenings just as it took take an act of Congress to add private Part C Medicare Advantage plans and the Part D pharmaceutical benefit.

Medicare is the only public program that is not based on income. Everyone over 65 is eligible for Medicare regardless of their income unless they immigrated to the U.S. after age 65 and did not work here. Everyone receives the same Part A benefit no matter their income. People must apply separately for Medicare Part B coverage and are penalized financially if they do not choose Part B when they initially apply for Medicare. Medicare "supplemental" plans charge a monthly premium and there are multiple options. Medicare Part C coverage differs depending on the insurer and as does Part D coverage.

People with disabilities who cannot work are eligible to apply for Medicare/Social Security Disability benefits. The application process, however, can take over a year leaving those who need assistance with daily living costs stranded. Medicare Disability Coverage can cover living expenses lost from an accident an illness or a disability. Such non-medical expenses are not covered by health care insurance companies. Little coverage for loss of living expenses is available except through some life insurance policies and worker's compensation or through the Veterans Administration, up to a limit.

Costs now overwhelming seniors are services not covered by Medicare such as long-term care and extended nursing home stays. For additional and specific information on Medicare policies and coverage see the Medicare Handbook: *Medicare and You* published by the Center for Medicare and Medicaid Services (CMS) or call the state Insurance Commissioner's office.

MEDICAID

Medicaid is designed to serve low-income individuals and families. Until the Affordable Care Act Medicaid only covered women and children. It did not cover low income males. Medicaid is a shared responsibility between the federal government and each individual state. The federal government defines a core set of benefits and gives the states a financial match based on the federal poverty level and income limits defined by each individual state. States can decide if they want to pay above the federal poverty level and receive matching funds to do so. They can also expand benefits.

The Affordable Care Act offered states a financial incentive to expand Medicaid. As of this writing, over 50 percent of the states have expanded their Medicaid coverage. Medicaid coverage by states can vary by month or week or the political make up of the governor and the state legislature. Consequently, coverage changes frequently. Medicaid coverage is restricted to permanent residents and US citizens.

Trying to describe Medicaid policies sounds as if people are speaking in tongues. The description goes: "People who are eligible must be at 100 percent or 150 percent of poverty." The federal poverty level is $23,850 for a family of four. If a family of four earns $23,850 then they are at 100 percent of poverty. This means that anyone at or below 100 percent of poverty is eligible. In 2014, the federal poverty level for an individual was $11,670 per year. State Medicaid programs can change the eligibility levels to 200 percent or more of the poverty levels or expand benefits. Consequently, any Medicaid discussion is terribly confusing to those who are uncertain whether they qualify for Medicaid or not and what Medicaid actually covers.

Another problem is that some states are richer than others. To make the program work financially states set the rates they will pay doctors for services. States can also raise or lower access services depending on the percentage of poverty level of the people they cover, such as 100 percent or 200 percent. Medicaid benefits differ by state and the poverty levels a state will cover.

Poverty rates however are defined annually. State budgets are also adjusted each year or every other year depending on the state.

Because many states pay lower rates for Medicaid patients many doctors, especially specialists, will not accept Medicaid patients because they are paid less than they are for privately insured patients. Medicaid patients often have more complex care needs because of their limited access to health care services and the effects of poverty.

The Affordable Care Act currently funds Medicaid expansion with taxes on hospitals. The logic is that with more insured people fewer people will need charity care at hospitals thus reducing a hospital's costs. This tax is currently under fire and may be eliminated.

The federal government covers nearly 60 percent of all Medicaid costs.

Because Medicare and Medicaid represent such a large share of health care expenditures their coverage and payment policies have a significant ripple effect throughout the system. It is simply easier for commercial insurers to mimic their coverage than to define their own. This is why physicians, hospitals, pharmaceutical manufacturers and others focus such intense lobbying efforts at the national level. Lobbying for rates, regulations, pharmaceutical benefits, medical devices and other covered benefits, such as colonoscopies or Hepatitis C drugs, for example, are intense.

Rate and coverage decisions provide a virtual road map for the private commercial insurance market.

PHARMACEUTICAL COMPANIES

The pharmaceutical industry has the highest profits of any industry in the country—more than the financial world such as banks and investment companies. In 1999 pharmaceutical profits as a percentage of revenue were 18.6 percent—ranking higher than commercial banks. Commercial banks, the second top performing industry, had a 15.8 percent profit.

By 2013 according to *Forbes* magazine some pharmaceutical company profits were as high as 42 percent.
(*www.bbc.com/news/business-28212223*)

Here is a glimpse of the pharmaceutical impact on national economies:

- Total global spending on medicines exceeded $1 trillion for the first time in 2014

- Global spending on prescription medicines is expected to increase by $205bn-$235bn in the five years to 2017

- The US, EU5 (Germany, France, Italy, UK and Spain), Japan and China account for just under 70% of total global medicine spending

- In 2012 in developed economies, 72% of all spending was on branded drugs, with 16% on generics

- Spending on traditional pharmaceuticals in emerging markets is expected to rise by 69% over the next five years.

Source: IMS Health: www.imshelath.com/portal/site/imshealth

Pharmaceutical manufacturers are clearly for-profit. What is not said is that over every other sector of the health care industry—physician practices, medical technology, medical suppliers—is also for-profit. The exceptions are some health insurance companies, retirement communities, some nursing facilities and most hospitals which are largely not-for profit enterprises.

Pharmaceutical companies were banned from direct to consumer advertising until 1997. The pharmaceutical industry at that point moved from being just one player to being the dominant player. Just watch TV.

New cancer drugs and treatments can cost up to or over $100,000. One proton cancer course of treatment costs nearly $30,000 even though it has not been demonstrated to be more effective than other courses of cancer treatment that cost $18,000. The proton cancer machine was developed by and is owned by a venture capital firm.

Venture capital firm goals are to reap significant financial returns from their investments. Marketing is intense to drive physicians and patients to use treatments or medications that may or may not benefit from these products and services more than existing ones. A new focus for venture capital firms is not only medical devices, such as these machines, but also new high tech hospitals outside of America that benefit from the so-called 'medical tourism' because of the high cost of American health care.

Physicians are also paid by the pharmaceutical companies for speaking engagements, professional continuing education, and free samples among other things. Cut backs on pharmaceutical payments to the physician community are a major consequence of the Affordable Care Act. Physicians must now report income from these companies. Such reporting, however, is largely unnoticed by the public at large.

What is not widely known is that physicians even receive a commission on the use of certain chemotherapy treatments.

Ironically, hardly anyone in the health care industry has the information systems in place to do a cost-benefit analysis of the impact not only of these medications but nearly every other medical/surgical intervention or outcome as well. Almost everyone does 'Spin City' without sufficient data to prove or disprove the health and/or financial impact of various approaches.

As more attention is paid to quality and outcomes more light will be shed on these issues.

The major advantage the pharmaceutical industry and to large extent the medical device industry have over most other health care services and products is that their prices have remained outside Medicare and Medicaid's rate structures. The company sets the rates and the FDA approves the drug, then decides what portion of that rate Medicare will pay.

Medicare is also specifically prohibited from negotiating rates with pharmaceutical companies. Rate negotiation is left to individual insurance companies that lack the size and negotiating power of Medicare. In short, when it comes to Medicare the pharmaceutical company sets the price, wrestles with the FDA over cost, and pretty much has a free rein to charge what it wants without significant or meaningful rate control.

The fight about Medicare and prescription drugs, therefore, is a two-fold battle. One is cost the other is rate control. The pharmaceutical mantra is "no rate control." They don't bargain on cost. No insurer can match the bargaining power of public programs such as Medicare and Medicaid because of their sheer size.

The Congressman who led the fight for Medicare Part D legislation which prohibited Medicare from rate negotiation with pharmaceutical companies was immediately hired to head PhRMA (Pharamceutical Researchers and Manufacturers of America), the industry association of pharmaceutical manufacturers.

New pharmaceutical products are not tested against comparable products already on the market. New products are only tested to see if they are safe and effective. Additionally, clinical trials only consist of about one thousand people, most of whom are males, who have no other health conditions. Consequently, a drug's impact on a broader population that may have other conditions is not tested.

Some health plans do not allow a new medication on their authorized list until it has been on the market for five years to assess its long-term safety.

The fact remains—pharmaceutical companies not only have the some of the highest profits in health care they have some of the highest profits of any industry in the U.S. Americans pay far more for the same drugs than citizens of other countries.

References:

www.cancer.org/cancer/news/expertvoices/post/2013/02/20/is-proton-beam-therapy-for-prostate-cancer-worth-the-cost.aspx

oconnorreport.com/2013/06/special-report-worth-the-cost-and-benefit-drugs-and-devices-who-decides/

PUBLIC HEALTH SYSTEMS

Largely ignored by the private health insurance system is the public health system which includes not only the public health system, but also Centers for Disease Control and Prevention and many other agencies. Much of our health we take for granted is thanks to our public health infrastructure. State, county and city Public Health Departments assure among other things that our water is clean and that our food is safely handled in restaurants, sanitation, meat packing and food processing plants. It tracks diseases to prevent and contain epidemics such as flu, measles and ebola. In some cases, it offers services to people who otherwise cannot afford them. It doesn't have a marketing and public relations budget so most people never know what public health services do unless there is a potential outbreak of disease from natural disasters or unpredictable epidemics, such as HIV-AIDS, ebola, chicken flu and other contagious diseases, such as measles.

Probably no group has done more to assure the health and well being of all Americans than the public health system from clean water and sanitation to the eradication and containment of communicable diseases. Public health focuses on our health infrastructure that tries to minimize our health risks. They gather information about diseases, outbreaks, hospital admissions and deaths and collect and develop priorities for public health priorities. These priorities are largely ignored by the private insurance community.

Public health programs are funded by federal funds and by state and local programs. They examine the health of the community which hardly any other group does. This includes disease patterns, prevention and early interventions. They are, however, generally at the bottom of health priorities and federal, state and local funding, except in cases of emergencies. Consequently, their funding is constantly precarious.

COMMUNITY HEALTH CENTERS

There are other public programs that treat people who are on Medicaid or who have no other public or private insurance. The community health centers provide access to primary medical, dental and behavioral health care in local communities. They treat all patients regardless of their ability to pay.

Each independent center has multiple sites. There are over 180 centers in Washington state alone.

Community health centers receive funds from insurance and reimbursement from public programs, as well as from grants and private donations. They also provide culturally sensitive care given the wide range of the clientele they serve. Their team-based approach and 'medical home' approach to care is being tested by other private and public practices as a result of provisions in the Affordable Care Act.

Many businesses know these community centers play essential roles in the community health. Businesses and individuals, however, largely support only one community health center not the entire network in a given county or state. Because a majority of their funding comes from public insurance and federal grants their funding is often at the mercy of Congress, state legislatures and city and county elected officials forcing them to compete with other public agencies for scarce tax dollars. Private fundraisers augment their budgets but their geographic locations often impact the amount of funds they receive.

Community health centers in states that have expanded their Medicaid programs expect to see a reduction in uninsured patients, but regardless of that expansion or not they anticipate continuing to serve patients in their local communities.

MILITARY HEALTH AND THE VETERANS ADMINISTRATION

In addition to the private commercial insurance market for employers there are specific programs for the military. Many military bases had their own hospitals and clinics but as the military grew in size many local military facilities could not handle necessary services. Congress consequently created CHAMPUS which has now evolved into TRICARE. TRICARE provides health services through private insurance companies for active and retired military personnel and their families. It also includes some reservists. In the early 2000's it added a long-term care component that was not previously available.

The Veterans Administration (VA) gives preference to service related disabilities and illness. Others may be treated on a space available basis. The VA has it own facilities and medical personnel. To receive services veterans must use VA facilities which are often located far from where many veterans live. The scandal over backlogs and distance led to the new Veterans Access, Choice and Accountability Act of 2014 that allows veterans who live over 40 miles from a VA facility to seek care from civilian providers. Some facilities can be as far as 200 miles or more from where a veteran lives. As the number of wounded veterans has increased from the Korean, Vietnam, Gulf Wars, Iraq and Afghanistan, access to quality care has become a major issue in health care policy, budgetary debates and funding.

Lack of adequate VA resources leaves many veterans vulnerable and homeless. It is estimated that one in four veterans is homeless.

TRICARE and the Veterans Administration are exempt from the Affordable Care Act.

INDIAN HEALTH SERVICE AND URBAN INDIAN SERVICES

A truly neglected sector of the US health care system is health care for American Indians and Alaskan Native (AI/AN). Health care was often included as part of the treaty agreements between the US and Indians in the 19th century. In 1955, Congress created the Indian Health Service inside the Department of Health Education and Welfare. But over the years investment in tribal health care has eroded. In the mid 1990's AI/AN health was shifted to tribal management to implement the national AI/AN policy of self-determination established in the 1970's. This gave AI/AN greater control over health services, but with inadequate funding. Today tribes manage over half of the $4.3 billion Indian Health Services budget, but significant disparities remain.

Additionally, a growing number of Indians have moved from reservations to cities where health care access is problematic. While 71 percent of Indians live in cities, Congress has appropriated less than 1 percent of the Indian Health Services budget for urban assistance. Medicaid expansion was assumed to reduce their insurance premiums but historical and cultural differences continue to plague access to non-Indian health services often caused by racial bias that often results in delayed or inadequate care.

The few organizations that receive funds from the 1 percent allocated cannot meet the growing needs of urban AI/AN. The Affordable Care Act did not adequately address these needs. Agreements have seriously eroded. Local doctors and hospitals that were once reimbursed for Indians not eligible for tribal care have faced significantly reduced funding.

Funding from tribal coverage does not follow Indians to cities. Additionally, the tribal reciprocity agreements no longer exist. A Navajo from Utah, Arizona, or New Mexico visiting Washington state, for example, can no longer receive health care services from tribes in Washington state as they could before.

A new Urban Indian Health Care initiative is trying to address that growing need. The initiative is largely underfunded and invisible. While there are provisions within the Affordable Care Act for Indians, they too are largely invisible.

LONG TERM CARE AND NURSING HOMES

The stealth danger in the health care system is assisted living and long-term nursing home care. Assisted living, home health and nursing home costs and staffing are grenades waiting to explode. Salaries for nursing home workers are not on par with workers in other sectors of the economy. Indeed, workers in the pet care industry often receive more pay than personal care workers in senior care facilities or in home health care. Work in assisted living, adult family homes and skilled nursing facilities is hard work, involving lifting, bathing, feeding and caring for fragile and vulnerable people. People in these settings not only need health care services, they also need extensive social support services such as transportation and social engagement services to keep them mentally and physically engaged rather than sitting and staring at TVs.

The burden on caregivers, both family and others, is significant to arrange services, to tend to the person's needs, to provide transportation, pay bills, organize medications and to find respite for themselves. Such demanding care even for someone they love deeply often leaves caregivers at risk of personal and physical exhaustion. Respite is desperately needed, but not always available.

The elder care industry faces a cost and access crisis that pales in comparison to other health care sectors.

There are not enough nursing beds to meet the needs of the current senior population much less the boomers who are just turning 65—the age of Medicare eligibility. By age 75 most people have one or more chronic diseases and will face at least one to three years in some kind of assisted living or nursing care facility.

Over 70 percent of all Americans think Medicare pays for assisted living and long-term care. It does not.

Medicare only pays for limited skilled nursing facility stays—up to 100 days. It only covers this care if someone has been in a hospital first. This policy is based on the assumption the person will recover after a hospital stay and return home. Only Medicaid, private long-term care insurance or personal family funds pay for the kind of nursing care for people who have chronic diseases such as Alzheimer's Disease. Such diseases require personal care including dressing, bathing and eating. Personal care is not medical care and therefore is not covered by medical insurance.

Long-term nursing home costs are paid for either by family funds, by private long-term care insurance or by Medicaid. For Medicaid to cover long-term care costs people must meet Medicaid's asset test. Therefore individuals and families must show that they are living at or below the federal poverty level.

The federal poverty level for one individual was $11,670 in 2014.

Monthly dementia care costs can easily be $5,000 or more depending on the state and the facility. At this price family assets can rapidly dissolve. To avoid these costs and quality for Medicaid families try to transfer assets within the family so their parent or relative will qualify for Medicaid.

Reams of rules and regulations have been written governing "transfer of assets" to prevent people from giving their assets to other family members. Medicaid which covers long-term care has been the fastest growing sector of state budgets. Medicaid now accounts for nearly 20 percent of state budgets and is second only to costs for primary and secondary education.

In 2002 Mississippi considered eliminating 13,000 Medicaid nursing home beds to balance its state budget.

Everyone in the aging industry and elected officials know about this lurking crisis but nothing seems to change. Nursing homes, assisted living facilities and home health care agencies remain squeezed by rate cuts.

Even Continuing Care Retirement Communities that promised life-long care face financial problems because of longer life expectancy and increasing care costs. Assisted living costs in these homes are in addition to entry fees.

Other companies that once offered life-time long term care insurance are either going out of business or increasing their annual premiums by 15 percent or more because of increasing health care costs coupled with increasing longevity. Some companies even charge higher rates for single women because they have a longer life expectancy than men.

THERAPISTS: OCCUPATIONAL, PHYSICAL, RECREATIONAL, SPEECH

Access to therapists depends entirely on the benefit packages insurance policies that individuals buy. Medicaid has no consistent rules for these therapies. Medicare has some allowable services which can be extended with supplemental policies. The therapy names are grossly misunderstood by the public. Speech therapy has as much to do with cognitive rehabilitation as it does with talking and swallowing; occupational therapy deals with activities of daily living from bathing and brushing teeth to spatial relationships rather than work; recreational therapy can mean simple things like making change and navigating on buses to walking in the community rather than getting a hair cut or meeting friends for coffee. Physical therapy, while largely accurately named, also deals with fundamentals of memory, such as recalling exercise routines.

Medicare defines the length of coverage and depends on individual supplemental plan coverage to go beyond that. Medicaid relies on the levels of care each state decides. In some cases Medicaid Speech therapy only covers life threatening problems, such as eating and swallowing, not cognitive rehabilitation. Rehabilitation care is essential for physical and cognitive recovery or improvement, but is not considered to be an Essential Benefit of any significance in public or private insurance coverage.

Without such therapy many patients have little opportunity for a complete or more successful recovery.

MENTAL HEALTH, COGNITIVE DISORDERS, AND ADDICTION

The same cost and coverage issues apply to mental health coverage, cognitive disorders and addiction. Those issues are often relegated to some public programs or depend on family funds. Mental health may be covered on some insurance plans but usually at extra cost. Despite the overwhelming impact addictions have on health care costs and community health, addiction treatments remain very difficult to obtain. Addiction treatment is not always included in many insurance packages.

Some insurance packages will cover the costs of autism or attention disorders. When the child reaches school, however, the insurance company often denies individual coverage and leaves the responsibility to special education teachers in already under funded public schools. This creates a ping-pong game between the schools and the insurers about who has financial responsibility. Lost in the dust of the debate are the students and their families.

Mental health parity laws are changing some of these problems. The first mental health parity law passed in 1996. It banned annual and lifetime limits on mental health care. In 2008 Congress voted to close the loopholes that health plans had used of arbitrary caps on mental health treatment days, higher copayments, co-insurance and deductibles. The law was expanded to assure mental health services had no more restrictions than other medical and surgical benefits. The ACA also added that addiction coverage must be no different from medical and surgical benefits, but that impact remains to be seen.

Many states have 'boarding' practices that keep mental health patients within hospital halls until the patient is stable enough to be released. Many are often just released to the streets. Boarding is now prohibited in some states. Yet the problem remains that there are few places for the chronically mentally ill. State, county and city jails remain the major 'treatment' facilities for mental health patients.

It is estimated that 24 percent of all jail inmates, 14 percent of State prisoners and 10 percent of all federal prisoners have at least one mental disorder. Jail inmates have the highest rate at 60 percent, followed by state prisoners at 49 percent and federal prisoners at 40 percent.

INTEGRATIVE HEALTH CARE

Until 1911 naturopathic medicine, homeopathy and chiropractic care were considered part of US medical school curriculum. Most medical schools at the time were private for profit enterprises established by one or two doctors in conjunction with a local hospital. The disarray and quality of the medical curriculum, however, led to the need to standardize the medical curriculum if medicine was to be a respected profession. This disarray led to a national study and the Flexner Report that brought about the standardization of medical education. In the process it also eliminated naturopathic medicine and other practices from medical schools. Consequently, they were also excluded from insurance in the 30's with Blue Cross and Blue Shield, the country's first private insurance plans. People seeking such coverage since then have paid for those services from their own funds.

Interest in these integrative therapies or the so called CAM practices (Complementary and Alternative Medicine), has bloomed since the 1970's and has caused increasing pressure on insurance companies and employers to cover these services. Eighteen states currently license naturopathic physicians but only two states (Washington and Vermont) have statutes mandating insurance coverage for naturopathic services. In other states insurance carriers may opt to cover CAM providers but there is no requirement to do so.

Such coverage decisions are made by individual states. State coverage changes frequently and these numbers cannot be considered to be the final word and will most likely change as this book goes forward.

CAM therapies are not in the Essential Benefit package of the Affordable Care Act.

EYES, EARS AND TEETH

While vision and hearing examinations are included in most health insurance policies, non-surgical interventions are not. Therefore, eye glasses and hearing aids are usually not covered. Hearing aids and glasses are covered only in supplemental policies under Medicare and in most private insurance policies.

Dental care is virtually ignored unless surgical care is the result of an accident or congenital disorder. Dental coverage, including extractions, implants, and dentures are covered only by separately purchased dental insurance. Even on Medicaid dental coverage is not a standard benefit. Consequently many rotten teeth are not replaced which has a significant impact on a recipient's ability to work because of appearance. This significantly impacts a person's ability to live independently and be economically self-sufficient. Significant and life-threatening health issues may often arise from abscessed teeth and gum disease.

If dental issues are ignored treating other medical complications does little good.

ATTORNEYS AND MALPRACTICE

To many, no discussion of health care coverage and costs is complete without including attorneys and the fray over malpractice costs. If insurers and pharmaceutical companies are fingered as villains attorneys are not far behind. Often seen as necessary evils that turn the flaws of the system to some group's economic advantage they are often despised. Attorneys are targeted as the reason for health care costs increase because of lawsuits, malpractice insurance and potential lawsuits. This is not true.

Studies indicate malpractice accounts for barely a percentage point of overall system costs. Despite these views, every group from the health care industry to consumers hires them to introduce and lobby for bills they want passed by Congress, state legislatures and state and local governments. They are also hired to draft model legislation or to sue the government, insurers, or whomever. Whenever some group does not get its way or if a medical procedure goes drastically, permanently or terminally wrong lawyers are always brought in to save the day.

Attorneys are actually no better or worse than any other major player in a system that has created so many enemies or that uses oceans of money for lobbying or advertising.

They are both adversary and advocate.

INEQUITIES IN HEALTH

None of the above, however, addresses the pernicious, continuing and systemic problem of inequities in health based on race, ethnicity and poverty. In thirty years' time desegregation issues are still rampant in parts of the south and in non-southern urban cities. And so is access to care. Access to health care services is difficult at best for anyone in poor or rural communities. Public transportation is often an access issue. Finding quality health care is nearly impossible for rural black communities and poor communities/neighborhoods of color in large urban cities.

Significant problems exist as well for immigrant and ethnic communities because of poverty, language and cultural views of health. New hospital laws to promote financial assistance policies in local communities and the requirement that they be translated may address some of these pervasive issues.

DEATH AND DYING

The American culture has not been one that easily accepts discussion about death and dying. Nor does it address how to cover such care. Hospice and palliative care have only recently been part of a health care discussion. Coverage for end of life care, however, is sorely limited.

Hospice care has only recently been added as a Medicare benefit and in other insurance policies. To qualify for Hospice a patient must be determined by a doctor to have only six months to live. While becoming more flexible in its rules few people don't take advantage of the program and most don't enroll in hospice programs until quite late. The average time a person is in hospice care is two weeks when palliative care could have been available earlier and could have eased care for the family and made the patient more comfortable. A new book on end of life care by Atul Gawande MD *Being Mortal*, addresses the importance of discussing end of life decisions so our end of live wishes will be respected.

Many people also fail to prepare for their death or designate someone to have health care power of attorney. This means if they are injured and cannot speak for themselves no one can speak for their preferences in a critical life threatening circumstance. Consequently, people may receive care they do not want or are not treated because they cannot speak for themselves.

At the present time only two states have Death with Dignity laws as of this writing—Washington and Oregon. These laws permit a person to decide if their life has eroded to such a point that they no longer have the dignity or quality of life that is important to them. In Washington state two physicians are required to sign the forms that allow a patient to select such terminal care.

THE DECISION MAKERS

GOVERNORS

If there is any group in a position to make deals with all the major players in the healthcare industry it is state governors. They preside over their state budget which includes the health care benefits for state employees as well as Medicaid. In some states they appoint insurance commissioners. In other states insurance commissioners are elected. Governors arm wrestle with the federal government over Medicaid rates and coverage. Many do not want Medicaid expansion under the Affordable Care for largely political reasons.

Governors appoint boards that oversee the licensing of hospitals, doctors, nursing homes, and other health care professions and facilities. They wrangle with their state employee unions over health care benefits and costs. They work with other governors in Republican and Democratic governors associations as well as in the non-partisan National Governors Association where they all focus on health costs. They work with their legislatures to give tax breaks to some employers to keep or create jobs in their state. This also exempts these employers from state insurance premium taxes.

Governors must also balance the state's budget and must work with their state legislature to do so, which is often controlled by a different political party. This is a full time and complicated job because they are also accountable to state citizens and of course they must stand for re-election.

If any one group could influence change it would is governors. But they get caught in the same ideological war zones as Congress and the President. Nor do they agree on Medicaid benefits and structure or insurance rules and regulations with their fellow governors because health care benefits differ state by state. Yet all the states face the same challenge of growing long-term care costs as the baby boomers age often without adequate long-term care coverage which is most frequently paid by Medicaid from limited state budget coffers

They must also deal with the often competing interests of counties, cities, business communities and the electorate as well as the often competing demands of other state agencies and their budget demands, such as transportation and education.

Governorships are often the launching pad for Presidential campaigns if their track record has been successful. Governors wear many conflicting hats.

THE PRESIDENT, CONGRESS AND THE COURTS

While elected officials create the rules for health care they often wash their hands of responsibility. They often are too busy fighting and blaming each other for the gaps in our health care system to do much of any significance. When there are signs of progress as in the Affordable Care Act one side lines up against the other in ideological battles rather than working collaboratively to solve a very pressing economic and social problem for the country and is too often a "my way or the highway" approach which leaves thousands of hard working people captive to uncompromising points of view. Health care has been called the third rail of politics: "Touch it and die."

The President and Congress are too often trapped in ideologically and party-driven mine fields so that no progress can be made toward common solutions. Health care is often characterized as: "government-run/socialized" or "privatized/

marketplace" as if it were that simple. More often than not those making these decisions often have very robust tax dollar funded health care benefits and have no idea about the real tradeoffs American families face.

The Affordable Care Act is a case in point. Health care has been such a lightening-rod issue that FDR left it out of the New Deal for fear that that his New Deal would completely fail if health care was part of the legislation. Truman could not pass it. While Johnson was able to garner support for Medicare and Medicaid, Nixon's comprehensive national plan failed to pass before Watergate.

Republicans and Democrats have had essentially the same mantra for years when the opposition makes a proposal: "Not on my watch you don't." Not liking the terms and provisions of the Affordable Care Act, those opposed to it are taking the battlefield to the courts and introducing piecemeal legislation designed to gradually undercut the legislation as a whole. One piece of legislation can essentially undercut another.

Eliminating the individual mandate is one example. Affordable health care depends on everyone having coverage and the same core set of benefits. People can add more if they wish. Without a common risk pool and the same core benefits health reform will not work. Unless there is one shared standard insurance package the insurance companies will keep designing policies that serve the healthy and charge others more. Thus damning anyone who has a pre-existing condition, the poor and dooming many hard working people to 'job lock.'

The fact remains that by the time we add up the costs of Medicare, Medicaid, Veteran's Administration, Public Health, National Institutes of Health, the CDC, the FDA, the Federal Employees Benefits program, military health, the robust tax funded Congressional benefits, and all the separately federally funded and state and local programs, federal, state and local dollars already probably account for nearly 50 to 60 percent of all US healthcare services.

As the Medicare program expands with the steady influx of aging baby-boomers—that percentage will grow.

We ignore health care reform to our peril. Our quibbling is just arranging deck chairs on the Titanic. Like medieval monks we have been reduced to debating how many angels can dance on the head of a pin while our health care cost and access plague rages around us.

OTHER PLAYERS

A complete list of other interests, providers and policy groups is virtually interminable: social workers, medical technicians, medical transcriptionists, allied health professions, laboratories, medical devices and equipment, software and information technology, home health agencies, professional associations ranging from physicians and hospitals to consumer agencies and even voluntary programs that offer services and education, such as the American Cancer Society, Heart Association, among many others. There are even venture capitalist groups that specialize in the health care industry for their own economic reward.

Numerous other groups focus on health care from programs within the National Institute of Health, academic institutions, private foundations, and professional associations, such as the Association of Health Care Journalists, among many others, not to mention private foundations.

Health care represents nearly 20 percent of the entire American economy. Turning this ship of state will not be easy.

Longer more thorough books have been written on this subject. There is much more depth than this quick guide. All this guide is designed to do is to give a quick, concise overview of a terribly and unnecessarily complex system and costly system.

But, wait! We have forgotten someone!

PATIENTS, FAMILIES AND FRIENDS—
"CONSUMERS" AND "BENEFICIARIES"

Patients continue believing they will get the care they need when they need it. Some even believe their insurance will actually cover their costs. They remain surprised when they learn that their insurance policy does not cover what they need. This includes Medicare and Medicaid and even the VA.

Health care remains a point-the-finger and blame-game battle field. Employers and insurers say patients want the highest levels of care, demand a no-holds-barred coverage for procedures and tests and demand all the heroic measures in the world, damn the cost when they are in fact terrified by the costs and safety. Doctors say patients want too much of their time and rely too much on quack information from the Internet. Hospitals want patients in and out as soon as possible but they also want patients to use their diagnostic equipment, have babies at their hospital and use their outpatient services. Insurers want patients if they are healthy and want doctors to see as many patients as quickly as possible. Doctors want to see patients and use their offices as well as their out-patient facilities. So on and so forth.

Congress, presidents and state and local elected officials only pay attention if groups and individuals make contributions or can influence voting blocs.

This is not a level playing field. Sick and hurt people are not "consumers" or "customers." They cannot shop voluntarily and their choices are limited by their insurance. They have little to no price/quality information for the "best deal" for a knee or hip replacement, a bargain colonoscopy, cancer treatment, or even the type of cast for a broken arm. Whose judgments do they trust? They have to use the provider their insurance covers. It is that simple.

There are few if any free choices.

As patients we are not in a position to discuss what kind of virus we have/don't have and which drug will be most effective or its impact with other medications we take. Most medical conditions and treatments are not "optional" if we want to get better.

Add to this confusion the stark reality of bankruptcy figures from health care costs: *Over 43 million people face medical bankruptcy, credit card debt and home foreclosures from medical costs. This is more than the combined populations of Illinois, Pennsylvania and Ohio.*

The bodies on this health care battlefield are entirely too real. They are ours. The truth is we no longer have time with our doctors. We are told what doctors we can see and for how long, what medications they can or cannot prescribe, what hospitals we can use, how long we can stay in the hospital, and what services are covered.

Patients have few powerful advocates or allies. We are trapped between Republicans and Democrats, yet both Republican and Democratic patients face the same heart wrenching dilemmas of how to pay for their long-term care or for some medications and treatments that cost over $100,000 or more. Cancer is not a partisan disease.

Most of us simply want access to safe health care services for ourselves and our loved ones without bankruptcy when we are seriously or terminally ill. Too often we are treated like huddled masses migrating between jobs and benefits when all we want is respect, safe, effective and affordable care.

WHAT WE CAN DO
ON THE ROAD AHEAD

We have no vision for the health of our nation. We have too many different rules, too many players at odds with each other and absolutely no incentives for anyone to work together. The economic survival of one group often means economic harm for another. No amount of tinkering will fix this non- system's fatal flaws. We must have systemic change.

Without such change we will drown in reams of differing rules and regulations and devour ourselves in meaningless diatribes about public options or medical savings accounts. We can change this system, but it will take work. Parts are already underway and making an impact. Many of the positive changes, however, are behind the scenes and are not 'sexy' enough to be "news." These positive changes include:

- Reports on economic ties between doctors and pharmaceutical companies.

- New annual fees on pharmaceutical manufacturers and medical devices

- End of lifetime financial limits on insurance policies for individual and families

- Limits on insurance company overhead and profits

- Fines on all hospitals for unnecessary readmissions, poor patient outcomes and fines for infections that came from hospitals where patients were treated

- New $50,000 fines and potential loss of non-profit status for hospitals that fail to engage the community in health care needs assessment and fail to create strategies to meet those needs

- One medical bill that combines hospital and physician fees for surgeries

- New patient care initiatives that stress value and outcomes over volume

- Tax credits for small businesses that provide health care benefits

- Public reporting of quality and outcomes by hospitals and publicly report fines for poor quality care

- Public reporting of ownership, accountability and expenditures by skilled nursing facilities

And much more.

MY CONCLUSION

Our health care system does not work. It does not work for individuals, families, many businesses, even many in the health profession who cannot or will not speak out. I can.

If there is duplication and redundancy in this book it is because the system in redundant and riddled with gaps and duplications and agencies with mind numbing rules, regulations and paper work.

Still worse are deaths and medical errors. Nearly 400,000 die annually from medical errors at a cost of nearly $1 trillion according to the National Patient Safety Foundation in testimony to Congress in July 2014. (*www.healthcareitnews.com/ news/deaths-by-medical-mistakes-hit-records*)

We always hear about the miracles and wonderful success stories, like mine. There is no comparable voice for those lost or destroyed in the bowels of cost, safety and errors.

No one is willing to face our system's failures just as families often fear the elephant in the room of addiction. Our health care system is our elephant in the room.

Here are conclusions I have come to:

- We need one risk pool and one set of common benefits. This will free unnecessary and expensive administrative costs. Large employers can add more if they wish but not at the expense of entrepreneurs, families, small businesses, the poor, the old, self employed and individuals. We should not have to fear starting, leaving or losing our jobs because of health care

- We must reward safety and quality and hold those accountable who fail to do so
- We need clarity in our bills so we can understand the actual costs
- We need innovation but not at the expense of compassion
- We need to compare new devices and drugs against what is on the market not just accept the newest potentially profitable patented tweak

Until everyone plays by the same rules and has the same access to the same core benefits without incomprehensible regulations we are lost. The Affordable Care Act is not perfect, but it is the best chance we have had to finally gain a health care system that works for us, not special interests.

WHAT YOU CAN DO

If you want safe and affordable care then advocate for quality and safety reports. Ask your hospital about its community needs assessments and how you can participate. Tell your elected officials that you want demonstrable quality and safety standards and reports and comprehensible rules and bills. Vast amounts of money depend on our system's complexity to preserve this lucrative status quo.

Your voice counts in your community and with your elected officials. You vote. You can act. Or not. It is your choice.

But, if you do nothing your money and mine will continue to go to very deep special interest pockets.

Their interests are not ours.

It is your choice.

A QUICK HISTORY OF U.S. HEALTH CARE REFORM

Benjamin Franklin starts insurance for fire protection. Insurance not considered commerce and therefore not subject to federal regulation

- 1752—Benjamin Franklin founds insurance industry with Philadelphia Contributionship of Houses from Loss by Fire.

- 1851—New Hampshire appoints first insurance commissioner.

- 1869—in *Paul v. Virginia* Supreme Court decides "issuing a policy of insurance is not a transaction of commerce." States have responsibility for taxation and regulation of insurance.

- 1871—National Insurance Convention formed. Now National Association of Insurance Commissioners.

- 1911—Flexner Report standardizes medical school curriculum and eliminates naturopathic health and related providers, such as homeopathy and chiropractic. Medical schools for medical doctors only.

- 1912—Teddy Roosevelt advocates for health care reform but defeated because called 'Socialist.' Major opposition from life insurance companies.

- 1929—1932—Committee on the Costs of Medical Care formed. A private national commission created by AMA to examine ways to control health care costs and prevent bankruptcies for American families. Funded by private foundations not government funds. Committee proposed having salaried doctors and community health planning. Failed with major opposition from AMA.

- 1929-1930s- Blue Cross and Blue Shield insurance companies formed to save hospitals and doctor practices during the Depression.

- 1942—1950's—Wage-price freeze. War Labor Board rules wage price controls do not apply to fringe benefits, such as health care. National Labor Relations Board rules that employee benefit plans are subject to collective bargaining. Health care benefits allowed as compensation during WWII wage /price freeze. Beginning of health care as a form of employee compensation. FDR administration.

- 1943—Supreme Court decides physicians may legally be salaried opening door for group practices, coops and physician owned clinics.

- 1944—Supreme Court in *U.S. v. South-Eastern Underwriters Association* decision declares insurance is commerce and therefore subject to federal regulation and oversight.

- 1944—Science promoted as basis for medical school curriculum after success in WWII focus on curing diseases and trauma care.

- 1945—Congress enacts McCarran-Ferguson Act and gave states continuing authority to regulate and tax insurance and declared that state regulation was in best interest of consumer. Insurance exempt from federal anti-trust laws. This act over turned the 1944 Supreme Court Southeastern Underwriters decision that made insurance regulation subject to federal regulation.

- 1945—Truman calls for national health insurance with voluntary fees. Killed by AMA.

- 1954—IRS rules health care insurance offered by employers is exempt from taxation.

- 1960—Kennedy proposed health care services especially for the elderly. Effort failed.

- 1965—Johnson worked with Congress to pass Medicare for the elderly and Medicaid for the poor. Bill barely passed.

- 1965—Congress introduces "retrospective cost-based reimbursement" to pay hospitals at end of patient stay. Hospital costs increase.

- 1974—Nixon introduced comprehensive health care reform through employers and subsidies for everyone else. Failed.

- 1974—New wage price freeze leads employers to expand health care coverage in lieu of wages, during Nixon administration as originally occurred in FDR administration.

- 1974—Nixon introduces ERISA (Employee Retirement Insurance and Income Security Act) part of which exempts large employers from state insurance regulations.

- 1976—Carter proposes national health insurance, but it fails because of recession.

- 1985—Reagan introduces COBRA (Consolidated Omnibus Budget Reconciliation Act) allowing employees to pay for their own health care at company rate after leaving a company.

- 1988—Reagan introduces Prospective Payment System (PPS) including DRG (Diagnostic Related Groups) payments to hospitals to control health care costs. Leads hospitals to find outpatient services to get around DRGs for income.

- 1988—Medicare Catastrophic Care Act passed to add prescription drug coverage for seniors and coverage for catastrophic costs. Passed and repealed within one year by angry seniors.

- 1992—George H.W. Bush implemented Relative Based Scale Value (RBRVS) to adjust salary value for physicians to minimize differences between specialists and primary care doctors.

- 1992—G H.W. Bush calls for electronic medical records within one year.

- 1993—Clinton advocates for managed care to control health care costs and proposed universal coverage. Universal health care failed. Managed care drove up costs because of administrative requirements.

- 1996—Clinton—HIPAA (Health Insurance Portability and Accountability Act) to protect patient privacy in health insurance and assure guarantee issue for patients especially for AIDS patients.

- 1997—Clinton—Children's Health Insurance Program passed.

- 1997—Clinton introduces Sustainable Growth Rate (SGR's) to adjust physician salaries.

- 1999—Financial Services Modernization Act of 1999 also known as Gramm-Leach–Bliley Act repeals Depression era Glass-Steagall Act. Reaffirms that states should regulate insurance.

- 2003—GW Bush introduces Medicare Part C—Medicare Advantage, private managed care Medicare plans and Medicare Part D, prescription coverage. Medicare prohibited from negotiating rate with pharmaceutical companies—left to individual insurance plans.

- 2008—Hillary Clinton campaigns on national health insurance but loses to Obama.

- 2010—Obama administration—Congress passes Patient Protection and Affordable Care Act (PPACA or ACA) that focuses on quality, safety and outcomes for payment and requires all individuals to purchase health insurance or be fined. Hospitals fined for poor quality health care; new physician hospital arrangements Affordable Care Organizations (ACOs) reward providers for outcomes and value.

- 2010—ACA introduces essential benefits for all insurance plans, over time, including ERISA companies.

- 2010—Dodd-Frank Act creates Federal Insurance Office in Department of Treasury to collect and inform Congress on insurance regulation. Primary insurance regulation remains with states as decided by McCarran-Ferguson Act. Does not replace power of states to regulate and tax insurance. States responsible for solvency oversight and regulation of insurance marketplace behavior.

- 2011—Continuous attempts made to repeal or reduce ACA in courts and by Congress.

- 2012—Supreme Court declares ACA individual mandate and Medicaid expansion is constitutional, but expansion may not be forced upon the states.

- 2015—Current *King v. Burwell* Supreme Court decision announced in June/July. Other potential cases against ACA are in process of being filed, including potential employer coverage requirements over Cadillac Tax.

RESOURCES AND REFERENCES:

Medical Care For The American People, The Final Report, Committee on the Costs of Medical Care, University of Chicago Press, October 1932

Social Transformation of American Medicine, Paul Starr, Basic Books, Inc. 1992

National Association of Insurance Commissioners

Department of the Treasury. Federal Office of Insurance

National Bureau of Economic Research

kff.org/report-section/the-coverage-provisions-in-the-affordable-care-act-an-update-individual-and-employer-requirements/

New York Times, Financial Times, among others

SELECTED REFERENCES

EMPLOYER STATISTICS AND INFORMATION: PRIVATE AND PUBLIC

http://www.bls.gov/news.release/empsit.t17.htm

UNION MEMBERSHIP AND RIGHT TO WORK

http://labornotes.org/2009/02/uaw-agrees-givebacks-ford--Ford and UAW

https://www.unionfacts.com/cuf/vitals

PHYSICIAN PAYMENTS AND RBRVS AND SGR

https://supreme.justia.com/cases/federal/us/317/519/case.html Supreme Court decision permitting salaried physicians.

http://en.wikipedia.org/wiki/Resource-based_relative_value_scale

http://en.wikipedia.org/wiki/Medicare_Sustainable_Growth_Rate 1997

MEDICAL ERRORS AND PATIENT DEATHS

http://www.npr.org/blogs/health/2013/09/20/224507654/ how-many-die-from-medical-mistakes-in-u-s-hospitals

Shining a light: Leape Institute, National Patient Safety Foundation 2015

Number of Physicians and Hospitals

http://www.aha.org/research/rc/stat-studies/fast-facts.shtml
(hospitals)

http://www.statista.com/topics/1244/physicians/

Affordable Care Act fees on Insurance Companies and fees for insurers

http://www.naic.org/documents/committees_b_ha_tf_related_ docs_aca_fees.pdf

http://thehealthcareblog.com/blog/2012/02/04/does-obamacare- limit-profits-for-health-insurance-companies-in-your-state/

http://obamacarefacts.com/obamacare-health-insurance- premiums/

Dying and Costs of Dying

Being Mortal, Atul Gawande, 2014

http://www.cbsnews.com/news/the-cost-of-dying/

Bright Lights for the Affordable Care Act

http://www.bloomberg.com/news/articles/2015-02-19/obamacare- proving-not-a-burden-to-u-s-from-chipotle-to-wal-mart

Medicaid and State Spending and Subsidies

http://www.pewtrusts.org/~/media/Data-Visualizations/ Interactives/2014/Medicaid/downloadables/State_Health_Care_ Spending_on_Medicaid.pdf

http://www.nytimes.com/2015/02/22/us/flood-of-briefs- on-the-health-care-laws-subsidies-hits-the-supreme-court. html?emc=edit_th_20150222&nl=todaysheadlines&nl id=54404043&_r=0

CONVERSION FROM NON-PROFIT TO FOR-PROFIT AND
CHARITABLE ASSETS

*http://www.communitycatalyst.org/doc-store/publications/
conversion_and_preservation_of_charitable_assets_of_blue_cross_
and_blue_shield_plans_mar04.pdf*

HEALTH REFORM, BUSINESS GROUPS, FOUNDATIONS AND
OTHERS

Alliance for Health Reform: *www.allhealth.org*

Foundation for Health Care Quality: *www.qualityhealth.org*

Institute for Health Care Improvement: *www.ihi.org*

Washington Health Alliance: *www.wahealthalliance.org*

National Business Group on Health:
www.businessgrouponheatlh.org

Pacific Business Group on Health: *www.pbgh.org*

Leapfrog Group: *www.leapfrog.org*

Kaiser Family Foundation: *www.kff.org*

Commonwealth Fund: *www.commonweathfund.org*

Robert Wood Johnson Foundation: *www.rwj.org*

Consumers Union: *www.consumerunion.org*

RAND Health: *rand.org*

OTHER REFERENCES:

Social Transformation of American Medicine, Paul Star, Basic Books Inc., 1992

Medical Care for the American People, Final Report: The Committee on the Costs of Medical Care, University of Chicago Press. 1932

Unaccountable, Marty Makary, MD, Bloomsbury Press, 2012

Summary of the Affordable Care Act: Henry J. Kaiser Family Foundation:

http://kff.org/health-reform/fact-sheet/summary-of-the-affordable-care-act/

Insurance Regulation in a Nutshell, John Dembeck, Debevoise & Plimpton LLC, PLI Handbook Course Handbook

SELECT RECOMMENDED READINGS:

Selling Sickness, Ray Moynihan and Alan Cassels, Nation Books, 2005

Better, Atul Gawande, MD, Metropolitan Books, 2007

The Immortal Life of Henrietta Lacks, Robin Skool, Penguin Random House, 2010

Overtreated, Shannon Brownlee, Bloomsbury Books, 2008

One Doctor, Brendan Reilly, MD, ATRIA books, 2013

KATHLEEN O'CONNOR is a 30+ year health care consumer advocate, non-profit executive and author. Passionate about family and patients' voices, she sponsored a $10,000 contest with her own funds in 2003 to *"Build An American Health System."* The contest led to the creation of CodeBlueNow! *www.codebluenow.org.* The Honorary Board included four former governors, Republican and Democrat. She also crafted the *CodeBlueNow! Papers* which ran in *The Seattle Post Intelligencer* for 10 consecutive weeks. *http://oconnorreport.com/old/codeblue/vital-signs/codebluenow-papers-seattle-pi-series/CBNpapers.pdf*

Her books include *The Buck Stops Nowhere: Why America's Health Care is all Dollars and No Sense* (1ˢᵗ and 2ⁿᵈ editions); *Embracing Two Lives,* a memoir of her life with her son and *The Alzheimer's Caregiver, Strategies for Support,* University of Washington Press, 1987. Her articles have appeared in local and national consumer and health care publications, From *The Seattle Times,* to *Washington CEO* and many industry publications. Her first article appeared in *The Washington Post* in 1959 when her school was the first in Virginia to be successfully integrated.

She currently publishes the O'ConnorReport: *www.oconnorreport.com*